Sometimes Mommy's Sad

By Rebecca Fajt

Illustrated by Lizy J. Campbell

Published by

4 Paws
Games and
Publishing

Bruno, Saskatchewan, Canada

I0173415

Sometimes Mommy's Sad
Written by Rebecca Fajt
Cover Art and Illustrations by Lizy J. Campbell
Edited by 4 Paws Games and Publishing
Formatted by 4 Paws Games and Publishing
Published First Edition
ISBN-13: 978-1-989955-01-7
Published by 4 Paws Games and Publishing
P.O. Box 208 Bruno, Saskatchewan, Canada S0K 0A0
http://www.4-Paws-Games-and-Publishing.ca
Publishing logo and name copyright © 2016 All Rights Reserved

" Dedicated to all parents experiencing postpartum depression and their children."

I know she has feelings, just like you and me

But sometimes I forget she does because she's my mommy.

She smiles when I'm happy and holds me when I'm sad

And I know if I write on walls it makes her pretty mad!

She teaches me to potty and how to comb my hair

So I can do it by myself and wear big underwear.

When I look in the mirror sometimes, I see my mommy's face

With eyes of the same colour and dimples in one place.

We both like French fries, dancing and watching our cartoons

And cuddling up in mommy's bed when I wake up too soon.

I watch her put on makeup; she always does it great

But I get lipstick on my nose, she just can't catch a break!

Mommy's her own person, she does her own things too

I like the colour pink, but she likes the colour blue.

I have short hair, she has long

And we have our own favourite songs.

Sometimes I get scared when she's gone and far away

But I know that the time will come to see her soon again.

As long as she is with me, she'll always teach me things

And we'll still love each other, despite our differences.

www.ingramcontent.com/pod-product-compliance
Lightning Source LLC
Chambersburg PA
CBHW042120040426
42449CB00002B/114